A Dialogue with Jesus

A Dialogue with Jesus

Based on the Gospel of John

Adolfo Quezada

To Pat Roads,
who loves the Gospel of John.

All biblical citations are from the Third Edition of *The New Oxford Annotated Bible*, Oxford University Press, New York, N.Y., 2001, unless otherwise specified.

Preface

Jesus was a paradox.

He was a gentle man whose word was mighty. His life was brief; yet, his influence has persisted through the ages. He was a man, yet God lived and loved through him. He walked the earth; but his spirit dwelt elsewhere.

Jesus would spend the night in the hills communing with the Beloved of his soul; loving and being loved. At dawn, he would descend from the hills into the valley to offer the love of God to everyone whom he met in the marketplace of life. This was his mission: to proclaim the truth that every living soul is one with God.

Author's Note

I hesitated writing a book entitled *A Dialogue with Jesus* because I thought it presumptuous and even irreverent to do so. Yet, it occurred to me that I have prayerful conversations with Jesus all the time; and writing down a dialogue would be the same thing.

I chose to place the dialogue in the context of the Gospel of John because it is the most spiritual of the four gospels. I chose only verses in which Jesus is speaking and to which I could best relate.

In the beginning was the word, and the word was with God, and the word was God.

John 1.1

Very truly, I tell you, no one can see the kingdom of God without being born from above.

John 3:3

Your birth was precious, Jesus, as was mine and the birth of every living soul. Though I was born into the realm of God, which is love beyond love, my life experience and the influence of a world that encourages a self-centered approach to life, made me worldly and selfish. The realm of God was an interesting notion to me, but I could not relate to it. I don't know when or why my heart began to open, and the Spirit of God touched my soul. All I know is that my life began anew.

The wind (Spirit) blows where it chooses, and you hear the sound of it, but you do not know where it comes from or where it goes. So it is with everyone who is born of the Spirit.

John 3:8

I know that I cannot capture the Spirit in a bottle like I might a firefly. It is so elusive. One day, it dwells within me and my heart is selfless and awakened. Another day I feel so utterly abandoned. I am forced to go deeper into my soul where the Spirit has chosen to abide. The Spirit will not be taken for granted, nor will it be domesticated.

God is spirit and those who worship him must worship him in spirit and truth.

John 4:24

No matter where I go, Jesus, God is there waiting to receive me. Whether in a church, a mosque, or a synagogue; the Spirit of God abides there. Whether on a mountaintop or in a cave; the universal presence of God is there. I cannot objectify God; nor can I limit to one place that which is ubiquitous. My loving attention to God can be offered anywhere I am because God is anywhere I am. My respect, my reverence, and my devotion to God can be shown even in the most unlikely places because I find God in the most unlikely places. What matters most, is not the location of my rendezvous with God, but that my prayer be spiritual, not intellectual; and that it be grounded in truth.

*My food is to do the will of him who sent me
and to complete his work.*

John 4:34

You, Jesus, were sustained by assenting to and doing the will of God. Your purpose in life was to serve God in the world. You knew that God had sent you to awaken hearts and enlighten souls. You asked others to follow you and to help you with your work. Even now, your Spirit moves us to complete the work you started. I feel your energy of love and service coursing through my veins, invigorating me to do the will of God; and to serve where I am needed.

Very truly, I tell you, the Son can do nothing on his own, but only what he sees the Father doing, for whatever the Father does, the Son does likewise.

John 5:19

You, Jesus, are the Son of God, even as we are all the children of God. You are utterly dependent on God for everything you do; and we too are completely dependent on God for everything we do. Your words remind us that we are not self-sufficient. We must look to God to show us how to live and love.

Do not work for the food that perishes, but for the food that endures for eternal life, which the Son of Man will give you.

John 6:27

You, Jesus, are the Son of Man; you share our humanity and our basic human needs. You know about physical hunger, and you know about spiritual hunger. Your compassion moves you to nourish our body; your faith in God inspires you to nourish our soul. Your words sustain our belief in our oneness with God.

I am the bread of life. Whoever comes to me will never be hungry, and whoever believes in me will never be thirsty.

John 6:35

I hunger for intimacy with God. I thirst for divine love. You, Jesus, dare such intimacy with God, and you are the vessel of God's love. Feed my hungry soul; quench my thirsty heart.

It is the spirit that gives life; the flesh is useless. The words that I have spoken to you are spirit and life.

John 6:63

Your words, Jesus, speak directly to my soul. They speak to me of that which transcends my flesh and centers on the Spirit. Your words reveal to me the crux of life and the matrix of all being.

*My teaching is not mine but his who sent me.
Anyone who resolves to do the will of God
will know whether the teaching is from God
or whether I am speaking on my own.*

John 7:16

You, Jesus, have the words that touch our hearts and change our lives. Your words are inspired by God; and your inspiration becomes our light.

I am the light of the world. Whoever follows me will never walk in darkness but will have the light of life.

John 8:12

You, Jesus, are the light of my life. No matter how dark the night gets, you light my way. Even on the darkest day of my life, the midnight of my existence, the light of life was upon me. My son laid dying in a hospital bed while I prayed for him and for all of us who loved him. He died on the third day of our vigil. The light I needed and received that day was not to cast off the darkness that consumed me, but to see my way through the darkness to the other side of hell. Your Spirit, your light, and your compassion were there for me.

If you continue in my word, you are truly my disciples; and you will know the truth, and the truth will make you free.

John 8:31,32

We follow you, Jesus, because your word echoes the word of God. It leads us away from the web of mendacity, and liberates us to live by truth alone. The truth that your words make known to us is not about the facts, but about our oneness with God and with each other.

Very truly, I tell you, whoever keeps my word will never see death.

John 8:51

I keep your word close to my heart, Jesus. And yet, I know that one day I will surely die. And even when I die, my soul will live on in oneness with God.

We must work the works of him who sent me while it is day; night is coming when no one can work. As long as I am in the world, I am the light of the world.

John 9:4-5

You were aware of your imminent death, Jesus, yet your focus was on doing the work you were ordained by God to do. Even as your time on earth was ending, you knew that those who followed you then, and who follow you now, would carry on the work of God. While you were in the world, you were the light of the world. Even now, your Spirit and your word is the light of the world.

I came that they may have life, and have it abundantly.

John 10:10

It is not enough for you, Jesus, to awaken my heart to the closeness of God. Your Spirit awakens me to abundant love, abundant faith, and abundant life.

I am the good shepherd. The good shepherd lays down his life for the sheep.

John 10:11

Even as your word brought peace and hope into the world, Jesus, you were tortured and killed for having uttered it. Your love for all beings was stronger than death. Your Spirit of love sustains us yet.

I hear the voice of your Spirit in my heart, Jesus. Even when I would rather wander away from your flock, my heart brings me back to you. Eternal life – which is knowing God in the here and now – is not a reward for following you; it is the consequence of following you.

The Father and I are one.

John 10:30

You are one with God, Jesus, as we are one with God. Your word has taught us that. Our oneness with God is at the core of your message. It is the foundation of all that we believe.

I am the resurrection and the life.

John 11: 25

Your word, Jesus, has raised us from the grave of our insipid life, and has led us to a vibrant life with God. Your word has taught us to die to ourselves, that we may live in God.

Very truly, I tell you, unless a grain of wheat falls into the earth and dies, it remains just a single grain; but if it dies, it bears much fruit.

John 12:24

Your word, Jesus, speaks to us of the circle of death and life. Death gives rise to life, and life surrenders unto death so that new life may arise. And the circle of life remains unbroken. You, who lived the epitome of humanness, fell into the earth and died so that much fruit would be born.

Those who love their life lose it, and those who hate their life in this world will keep it for eternal life.

John 12:25

Your word, Jesus, is sometimes paradoxical; and at times bewildering; yet always, it invites us to rise above the trivial and mundane. Always, it leads us to that which is eternal. Life is precious and must be protected; yet, there is something even more precious than life. It is love. Love is God in our life. We are willing to lose our shallow life for the sake of a life of oneness with God and with all creation. Love emboldens us to live authentically, and to sacrifice ourselves, even unto death, for the sake of our belief.

Now my soul is troubled. And what should I say – "Father, save me from this hour?" No, it is for this reason that I have come to this hour. Father glorify your name.

John 12:27

You were so desperate, Jesus, and afraid. Your human instinct to survive made you brace against the horrific event that was about to happen. You did not want to suffer; you did not want to die. It was not God's will that you be crucified; it was the will of those who were threatened by your word. You were sent to let the truth be known. They could not grasp the truth. You accomplished your mission, though at a supreme price. Your life and your death manifested God.

The light is with you for a little longer. Walk while you have the light, so that the darkness may not overtake you. If you walk in the darkness, you do not know where you are going. While you have the light, believe in the light, so that you may become children of the light.

John 12:35

Your life, Jesus, was a flash of light that lasted but a moment, yet, illuminated the world like the sun. Those in your midst heard your word and were enlightened. You uttered the word that God put in your heart, and the children of light passed on what you proclaimed. The darkness has not gone away, and it never will; but your word lives on and your light illuminates our path toward God.

Whoever believes in me believes not in me but in him who sent me. And whoever sees me sees him who sent me.

John 12:44-45

Jesus, you reflect God into the world. We see you and we hear your word, knowing that it is the essence of God that we see, and the words of God that we hear. It is the Spirit of God within you in Whom we believe.

I have come as light into the world, so that everyone who believes in me should not remain in the darkness.

John 12:46

Jesus, the light you shed in my mind and heart brings clarity to my life. I do not believe in you because of miracles you have performed; rather, I believe in you because, even in the greatest darkness, your radiance illuminates my way.

I give you a new commandment, that you love one another. Just as I have loved you, you should also love one another.

John 13:34

Love is the lifeforce that emanates from God. Even our love for God is a reflection of God's love for us. Your word, Jesus, awakens the love of God within us that we share with one another. To love one another as you have loved us, we evoke a love beyond love that only God can give.

Do not let your hearts be troubled. Believe in God, believe also in me.

                                    John 14:1

Our faith in God and in you, Jesus, is not based on a belief that all will be well, because we know that life includes times of trouble, struggle, and grief. Rather, our belief is based on your word that tells us that, no matter how dark the night, the Spirit of God is with us always, and will help us through the night.

I am the way, and the truth, and the life. No one comes to the Father except through me.

John 14:6

We cannot reach God except through our humanness. You, Jesus, who are the epitome of humanness, show us the way to God. You, who are authentic in your humanness, have grasped the truth and have offered it to us. You, whose divinity is grounded in your humanness, are the life of God in the world. Your word tells us that we are as well.

Peace I leave with you; my peace I give to you. I do not give to you as the world gives. Do not let your hearts be troubled, and do not let them be afraid.

John 14:27

Your word, Jesus, has assured us that we need not be afraid because the presence of God is a constant in our lives. You have taught us that God sustains us through whatever comes our way. The peace you offer to us has nothing to do with the world, and everything to do with the presence of God in our hearts.

I am the true vine, and my Father is the vine grower. He removes every branch in me that bears no fruit. Every branch that bears fruit he prunes to make it bear more fruit.

John 15:1-2

I have been pruned by life, though not as radically as you, Jesus. You have born much fruit from the branches that were left to you. I have tried to do the same. It hurts to be pruned; yet, it is bearable and even comforting if it is God who does the pruning.

*You have already been cleansed by the word
that I have spoken to you.*

John 15:3

Your word compels us to cut away that
which is not life-giving to us or others.
As we cut away that which is dead; we
allow new life to grow within us.

As the Father has loved me, so I have loved you; abide in my love.

John 15:9

You love me, Jesus, with the love that God has given you. I accept your love; I dwell in your love; I live my life in accordance with your love. All things come to an end, except for your eternal love.

*No one has greater love than this, to lay down
one's life for one's friends.*

John 15:13

The sacrifices that come of love take on myriad shapes and sizes. You, Jesus, spoke the truth to those who feared the truth. You risked your very being in the name of God and were crucified and killed. Your life changed hearts; your death changed the course of history.

Abide in me as I abide in you. Just as the branch cannot bear fruit by itself unless it abides in the vine, neither can you unless you abide in me. I am the vine; you are the branches. Those who abide in me and I in them bear much fruit, because apart from me you can do nothing.

John 15:4-5

All living souls abide in one another, and we all abide in you, Jesus. It could be no other way because we are all one. And because we are one, we depend on each other to bear fruit. Apart from one another, we lose our fecundity.

I have said these things to you so that my joy may be in you, and that your joy may be complete.

John 15:11

You not only offer us the love of God, but also the joy that love engenders. Beyond delight, beyond happiness, beyond ecstasy, is the joy of abiding in the love of God.

Very truly, I tell you, you will weep and mourn, but the world will rejoice; you will have pain, but your pain will turn into joy.

John 16:20

You, Jesus, must have felt that same dreadful sorrow that your friends felt when the time came for you to say goodbye to them. There is no greater pain than to part forever from one's beloved. You were acutely aware of the profound grief that your friends would suffer; and you did your best to give them comfort. You understood that it was natural for them to mourn you. You must have cried yourself.

When a woman is in labor, she has pain, because her hour has come. But when her child is born, she no longer remembers the anguish because of the joy of having brought a human being into the world. So you have pain now; but I will see you again, and your hearts will rejoice, and no one will take your joy from you.

John 16:21-22

You, Jesus, understood that through the pain and through the pining, the sun would rise again, and your friends would be with you at a deeper level of existence. What joy they must have felt to know that your Spirit would be with them forever.

You will suffer in the world. But take courage! I have overcome the world.

John 16:33

The New American Bible, The New Catholic Translation, Thomas Nelson Publishers, New York, N.Y., 1971, p. 1167.

You, Jesus, suffered so much before you died at the hands of those who feared your word. Your friends were made to suffer too; you warned them that they would. You called on their courage to get them through the worst. You overcame the world by commending your life to God. This, we must also do. Whatever the source of our suffering, we do not have to bear it all alone. Though sometimes we may feel abandoned in our suffering; deep within, we know that God is with us always and forever.

I ask not only on behalf of these, but also on behalf of those who will believe in me through their word, that they may all be one. As you, Father, are in me and I am in you, may they also be in us, so that the world may believe that you have sent me.

John 17:20-21

You asked God to care for those who followed you and for those who would follow them. You knew that your Spirit had set the world on fire with the power of your word. You prayed that they and their posterity would believe in their oneness with God. This, above all, was your message to the world: that we awaken to the reality that God is in us as we are in God.

For this I was born, and for this I came into the world, to testify to the truth. Everyone who belongs to the truth listens to my voice.

John 18:37

You, Jesus, are the epitome of truth. Truth is not just the opposite of mendacity; it is the declaration of what is real, authentic, and genuine. You came into the world proclaiming the truth. Your word touched hearts and changed lives because what you said rang true to those who listened. Your word was real and it was grounded in real life. You spoke of lilies in the field and of your Father in heaven. You spoke of a God who loves us beyond measure and wants to be intimate with us. These were truths that revolutionized the world.

*Peace be unto you. As the Father has sent me,
so I send you.*

John 20:21

Your word brings peace to us. It comforts us and gives us hope. You brought us into intimacy with God. Your Spirit is with us now and forever. You awaken us to the dire needs of our brothers and sisters in the world and ask us to respond to them with our compassion. You inspire us to be who God intended us to be. You send us into the world to live a life of love.

…do you love me?… Tend my sheep.

John 20:16

Your sheep, Jesus, are all the living souls who have ever lived. You would have me tend to those who share my time in history, my place on earth, and my circumstances of life. You ask me to love them as I love you; to serve them, listen to them, care for them, watch over them, stand by them, and, in all ways, be tender toward them. All this I will do, with the grace of God.

Follow me.

John 21:19

What has come into being in him was life, and the life was the light of all people. The light shines in the darkness, and the darkness did not overcome it.

John 1:3-5

Also by Adolfo Quezada

A Grief Revisited

Old Soul, Young Spirit

Praying to an Unknown God

Before the Night Comes

Love is My Religion

Return to Silence

Teaching Minds, Touching Hearts

A Spiritual Soliloquy

Spiritual Repose

Attention: A Gift of Love

Passages of Faith

My Soul in Winter

Jesus: A Story of Love

One with God

Light and Shadow

These and other books by Adolfo Quezada may be ordered through Amazon.com

Adolfo Quezada is a retired counselor and psychotherapist. He lives in Tucson, Arizona.